Ratboy, Etc.

Poetry by Michael Hathaway

Illustrations by Wayne Hogan

A Friends of the Frogs Award Edition

Kings Estate Press, 1994
870 Kings Estate Road
St. Augustine, Florida

—ACKNOWLEDGMENTS—

All of the poems in this book except "Karen Carpenter," "Aunt Irene," and the Ratboy poems were published in a very limited edition chapbook entitled *excerpt* (Mutated Viruses, Chicago, 1989). Some of the poems in this book have previously appeared in or been accepted by the following magazines or books: *Alchemist Review;* Big Head Press broadside series; *Chakra; Come Winter & Other Poems* (Plowman Press, Canada); *Crocodiles in Paradise* (Northwoods Press); *Dog River Review; Famous Last Words; For the Birds* (Samisdat Press); *Girder; God Poems* (Mulberry Press); *Great Bend Daily Tribune; Green Guts; Gypsy; Hyacinth House; Mutated Viruses; National Gay & Lesbian Reader; 1989 Dan River Anthology* (Northwoods); *Off My Face; one hundred suns;* One Tree Press postcard series; *Pearl; Pet Gazette; The Plowman* (Canada); *Poesflesh; Poetry Magic; Poetry Peddler; Poetry Rendezvous — A Book of Poems* (Great Bend Public Library, 1989, 1990, 1992 and 1994); *The Poet's Perspective: A Literary Capsule; Potpourri; Prairie Smoke: The Pueblo Poetry Scene, 1979-1989* (Pueblo Poetry Project); *Proof Rock; Ransom; RFD: A Country Journal for Gay Men Everywhere; River Rat Review; Silver Wings; Thirteen; Voices Poetry Magazine; Waterways: Poetry in the Mainstream;* and *Wheels* (Germany).

Poems copyright 1994 by Michael Hathaway, 522 E. South Ave., St. John, KS 67576-2212

Illustrations copyright 1994 by Wayne Hogan, P.O. Box 842, Cookeville, TN 38503. All rights reserved.

ISBN: 0-9637483-4-3

Special thanks to Jane Hathaway for her help with the production of the book and to Shon Fox for the inspiration.

KINGS ESTATE PRESS
Ruth Moon Kempher, Editor
870 Kings Estate Road
St. Augustine, FL 32086

FOREWORD

Michael Hathaway is never one to trim life's corners to make them more palatable and sanitized. This is so true of this fine collection, the first substantial one, by this gifted young poet. He writes with a refreshing (sometimes brutal) honesty of lovers, sexual attraction, and of family and friends. He is detailed in reporting events and their settings. Here, in one of the impressive moments in the "Ratboy" sequence, he has an encounter with a vivid and bizarre youth who enters the poems taking all he can for his material, emotional and physical needs. The night, a wild one of drinking and frolicking, winds off at 3 a.m. when the speaker, exhausted, gazes about the room. He sees the spent beer cans and empty liquor bottles, trophies of a wild physicality reflected in the energy of the writing itself:

> wrestling and fighting ...
> slamming each others' heads against the walls,
> power pillow fights, broken lamps,
> busted ribs, jammed fingers, fistfuls of hair,
> teeth marks from head to toe,
> beer fights which saturate our clothes,
> back flips from one bed to another...

An image of his grandmother's face appears, as do her wonderfully "stern words": "'never set anything on top of a Bible.'" He rises, removes the Southern Comfort from the motel room Gideon Bible, knowing that Grandma, in Heaven, is smiling down "approval." The mix of the erotic drama, played out, is tastefully resolved in that final image — one that bespeaks the refreshing absence of any guilt throughout the book over Hathaway's gay self — even meeting rejection and frustration he feels healthy. He is a "doer," a poet and a publisher of one of the best poetry magazines going, *Chiron Review*. In the lyric "discarding," he rejects those who talk suicide, "suck smoke," and allow private bitterness to dominate their lives:

> i discard those who let skies
> fall on them, never blinking,
> those who fight star logic
> and dream magic with ignorance,
> prejudice, pessimism ...
> i discard years of hateful lying

A full, risk-taking engagement with life is Hathaway's central theme, and it helps him much that other people, "individuals" of variety and color, stimulate him. In one poem he risks a preacher's tone to make a point close to the bone: we "are not freaks" put on earth to be ridiculed. Our job is to forgive, not condemn. There should be "compassion" for every life we touch. And though Hathaway's spectrum is primarily gay, he celebrates the lives and loves of all of us with a largeness of spirit readers of this book will be nourished by.

Robert Peters
Huntington Beach, California
May 22, 1994

I.

Ratboy

**on sleeping together
literally, not figuratively**

handsome straight boy,
you said you wanted to sleep in my bed
but i couldn't touch your "o-zones."
of course i agreed,
having been touched by the way
you innocently handed me your heart
for safekeeping that night
in Gina's house in New York;
having been touched by your pretty smile
and laughing eyes which spark
with a hint of danger.
of course i agreed to anything
that would keep you close to me.

it's not that i want
to chain your soul to mine
or that i even need your touch,

it's simply this:
sleeping alone, i feel panic
when the black whale of night
opens its dark mouth
to swallow me whole.

but when you sleep beside me,
friend and kindred spirit,
poet/warrior/artist/songbird,
dancing, fun-loving soulmate,
the presence of your strength
is enough.

the presence of your tall brown form
sprawled out beside me
sleeping the sleep of the innocent
is enough—

even the soft sound of your steady
breathing is enough
to make the night safe,

night takes on new meanings.
i sleep;
peace tumbles from the heavens
into my dreams.

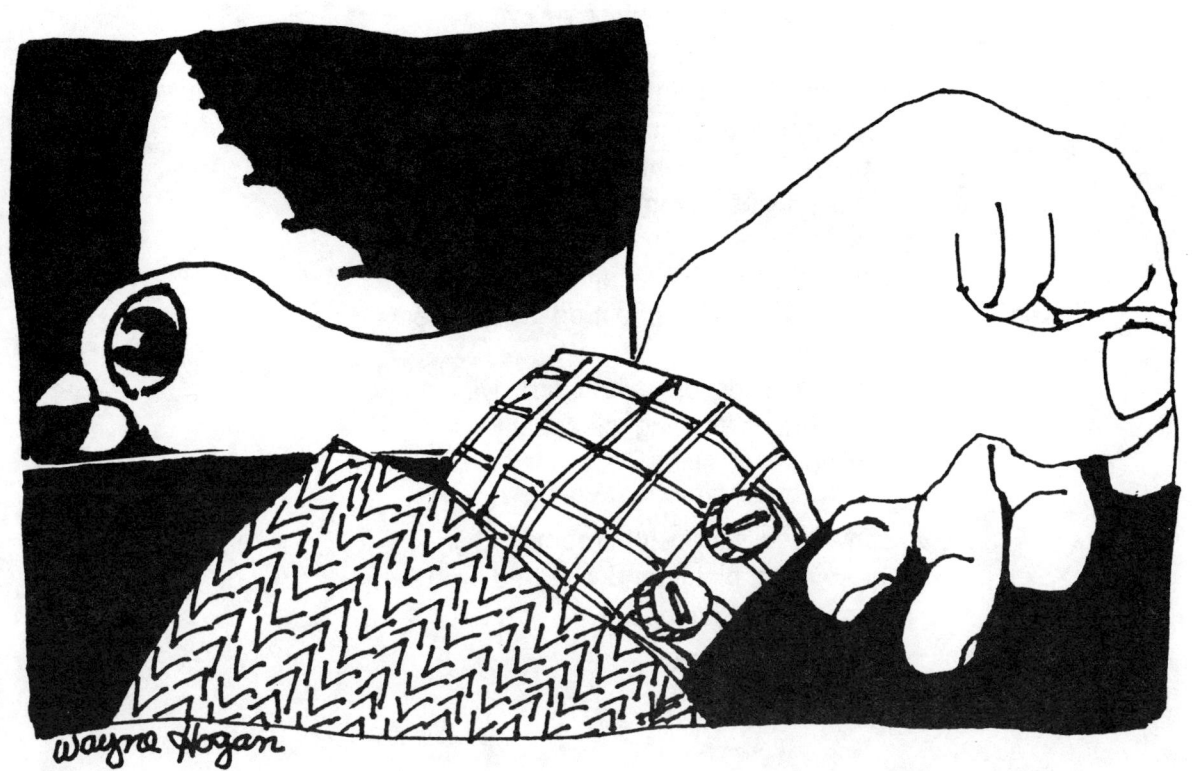

what would Grandma think?

every Saturday,
Ratboy and i jump into the car,
with a case of Keystone Light
and a bottle of Southern Comfort
and hit the highway
with no particular destination.

we find a town we think might be groovy,
rent a motel room and commence to enjoy
the finer things in life:

Diet Coke mixed lightly with
Southern Comfort,
beer chasers, delivered pizza,
Beavis & Butthead on MTV,

wrestling and fighting during commercials,
slamming each others' heads against the walls,
power pillow fights, broken lamps,
busted ribs, jammed fingers, fistfuls of hair,
teeth marks from head to toe,
beer fights which saturate our clothes,
back flips from one bed to another ...

3 a.m. finds us exhausted, lying there,
our brains floating pleasantly
in pools of alcohol.

my eyes scope the room:
i spy the nightstand covered with beer cans,
and bottles of booze.

Grandma's sweet face flashes before my eyes,
and her stern words:
"never set anything on top of a Bible."

i respectfully, carefully
remove all the beer cans
and the Southern Comfort
off the Gideon Bible,
pretty sure Grandma is smiling
down from Heaven in approval.

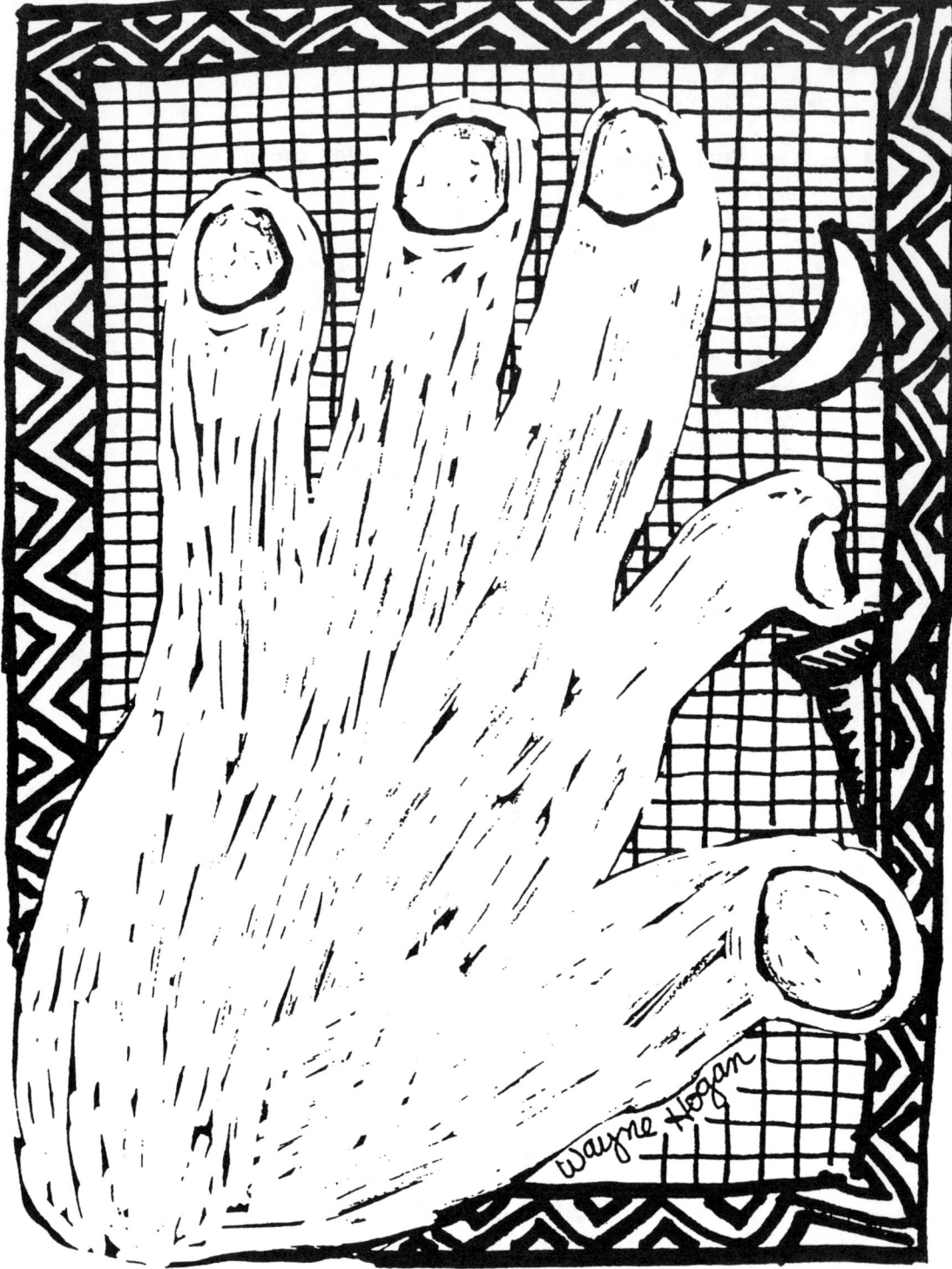

scrapper

he burst into town two years ago
from Dallas,
fists swinging, age 14.
he sought out the baddest, meanest
scrappers in town,
issued his challenge.
even when he lost, when it was over,
he'd sneer, "is that all you got?"

with so many demons to conquer,
full to the gills with Southern Comfort
sitting on my bed at 5 a.m.,
the story spills out of his mouth
about an eight-year-old boy
lying in bed in a trailer house
with his younger brother
while his mother and her boyfriend
scream and fight in the next room,
and this child must hold his hand
over his brother's mouth
to stifle the crying and whimpering,
"ssshhh! If he hears us,
he'll beat us, too."

on procuring a virgin for Ratboy

he left conveniently for a week
to spend his birthday with family
during the time we had to move
from the Stone Street house.
i told him, "don't worry Ratboy,
i'll clean up your thrashpit
(the basement where he partied)
and move your stuff."

i spent a lunch break cleaning down there.
the room was totally violated,
carpeted with hundreds of beer cans,
cigarette packages, butts and ashes,
dirty clothes, car stuff, poems,
treasured letters from poets,
condom wrappers, books, magazines,
perfumed letters from horny girls,
& some things were ruined by a sewer leak.

i emerged with armloads of trash,
sweat dripping off my face,
smelling like sewer water.

i moved our stuff into an
unsuspecting, clean motel room in Great Bend.

a week later he called and said
he would be home at 6 a.m. the next day.
i bought a case of Keystone Light,
a fifth of Southern Comfort,
a carton of Camel wide filters,
favorite cassettes, beef jerky,

a notebook, pens, artist sketchbook,
colored pencils, books, candy,
Playboy, Easy Rider, Mad Magazine,
a 12-pack of Mountain Dew,
any little thing i could think of
to make his heart sing.

i put it all in a basket.
waited up all night.
i said, "*WELCOME HOMF RATBOY!*"

i'm not a punching bag but...

he is stronger than me
and likes to hit

it is an art.
his eyes dilate,
his face gets a hard mean look,
he doubles his fist and swings wide,
brown biceps bulge

i like it,
the way it jars my whole being
that thud on my arm
or leg, or back, once in the eye
(you really do see stars)

the sheer male power behind the punch.
i never had that power,
it always mystifies, eludes me.

i like seeing it, feeling it,
understanding it

i take his touch, his skin
any way he offers it

it takes two

"I want to do something fun."
"Yeah, me too, let's go bowling. You pay."
"No, dumbass, I don't mean tonight!
I mean with my life, a career."
"Oh, you mean like me?"
"And what is your career?" I asked
my 17-year-old unemployed roommate.
"A bum, of course."
I contemplated.
Being sick of rising early each morning,
going to a deadend, boring job each day,
never having any free time
to do the things I love to do,
create what I love to create.
"Yeah! That's a good idea.
I've been a bum before.
I enjoyed it greatly!"
Panic crossed his face
as he attempted to restore order and logic
to our friendship:
"We can't *both* be bums, now, can we?!?"

*for all i know, all i'll ever
get from love is love songs*

our biggest fight to date was about music.
he was insane with anger when he had to
listen to my Carpenters' tape
and threw a ring-tailed hissy fit
and pouted during our California trip.
i didn't give in because i had listened
to Anthrax for him and it hurt.
we argued and ended up hitting
and strangling each other and
he even spit on the Carpenters' star
on the Hollywood Walk of Fame.

it was silly, but it still bothered me,
because to me, Karen Carpenter
was a goddess, an angel, a saviour,
one of the few pleasant memories
of my teenage years.
her music and voice were a beacon to me
since i was Ratboy's age.

i was sorry to upset him, but
this is what i say to Ratboy:

you know i've been on *top of the world*
ever since i first saw your
sweet sweet smile.

whenever you're away
there's a kind of hush all over the world
and *i won't last a day without you!*

and what do you do when you get hurt
or feel bored, the big emptiness taking over,
when your other friends turn on you?

you *run & find the one who loves you—*
and the one who loves you
happens to be the biggest
Carpenters' fan who ever lived.

it's something i'd only do for someone else

i ordered two tickets to a
WCW wrestling match in Salina
starring Sting, Rick Rude and Sid Vicious,
so Ratboy could be there in person
to watch giant men in tight briefs
pound and stomp the shit out of each other;
so he could see the blood and sweat
up close and personal;
so he could scream and jump
and join the bloodthirsty frenzy
of the crowd.

it was all worth it—
the tickets' cost,
sitting through the match—

for the smile
when i told him we were going,

the bearhug

i would do anything
to see that joy
taking flight in his eyes.

letter to Ratboy

i didn't know how attached to you i was
until you weren't here anymore.
the only evidence, a note saying,
"I joined the carnival."

your world is suddenly bright and colorful,
filled with the excitement you crave,
while mine is crashing around my feet,
color and meaning gone.

you followed me into every aspect of my life.
now everything and every place reminds me of you,
and they echo hard with your absence.
you pressed your existence into mine
so hard, so fast,
grasping for that soul connection,
you found it, made it click.

i remember the wrestling matches we had,
how ever careful you were not to hurt
my back and neck while you bodyslammed me
and tossed me about like a rag doll;
how you dashed out of restaurants and leapt
onto the hood of my car, standing there
victorious, 16, invincible,
always ready and able to conquer the world.

i want you to go, really.
have the grooviest summer of your life.
fly into the future,
embrace it dancing, singing, running,
and without looking back.

i smile, knowing that every place you go
will be glowing, alive with your young energy.
and everyone who meets you — man, woman and child—
will fall head over heels in love with you.

all i ask is that destiny is gentle
to your trusting soul,
that you are always safe and warm,
never hungry and never lonely.

and that if you ever tire of the road,
you might come home to me for awhile.

the club

when Ratboy ran off with the carnival
it was bad enough that it hit me hard
that he left a hole in my heart
bigger than my heart

i was inundated with heartbroken bimbos
ringing my doorbell: where is he?!?
when is he coming home?!?

the first one cried on my shoulder,
i tried to comfort her, said,
"you know he is a wild spirit,
no one can hold him. that's partly
why we love him, why we have to let him go."
she said gently, "i know you miss him too."
she left, tears glistening down her cheeks.

the second said sarcastically,
"do *you* know where he is?
he tells *you* everything..."
i said, "yeah, i know. he's flown head first
into the future embracing his destiny
with a big fat bear hug
and there's nothin' you nor i
nor anyone else can do to stop him."

the third was hysterical,
a brain-dead bug-eyed girl,
"where is he? where is he? oh gawd,
when is he coming home? i've been
crying for three days!!!"

i sneered,
"join the club, bitch!"
and slammed the door.

**my first love comes back
after i waited up all night
for you for the last time**

i'd been mentally bankrupt for months:
you never came home,
no sleep would come,
no poems would come.

but last night, three poems came at once,
today, one exploded onto my computer screen at work
before i knew what was happening.

now that the poems are coming,
i don't care
if you never come home again.

II.

Etc.

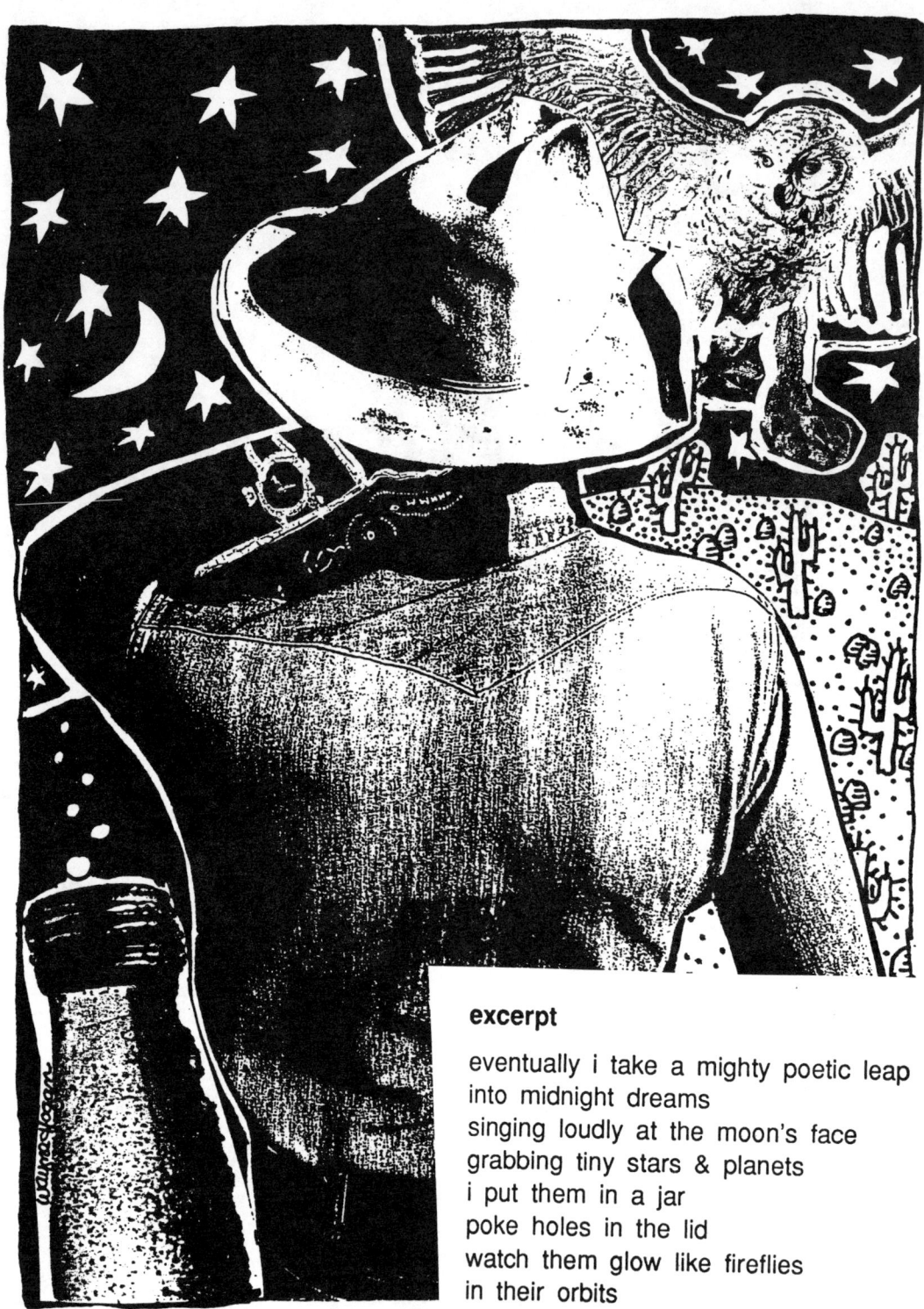

excerpt

eventually i take a mighty poetic leap
into midnight dreams
singing loudly at the moon's face
grabbing tiny stars & planets
i put them in a jar
poke holes in the lid
watch them glow like fireflies
in their orbits

nuclear poem

people seem annoyed
with thoughts of
human annihilation
as if this would be
the ultimate tragedy,
to have no human
living on earth.
but as much as i love
people sometimes,
i don't think earth
would miss us,
nor would the animals.
they were here first
anyway.
it would just be
quieter, cleaner,
more peaceful
when the smoke cleared.

a secret

i have a thousand books.
i buy them two, three, four
at a time
at garage sales, book stores,
thrift shops.
it's almost a mania,
i've been doing that
since i was 12:

history, religion, philosophy,
biography, archaeology, prophecy,
astrology, magic, nutrition,
psychology, mythology, poetry,
row upon row of classics,
paperback, hardback.

i don't read anymore.

but it seems like all the answers
to something
to everything
are there, lined up on those shelves.

i have all the answers in the world
waiting for me
in case i ever want to know.

discarding (1994)

i discard rotting shit
from my tired heavy orbit.
nothing is sacred:
every scrap of paper
     poem   photo
letter and song,
every memory that left
tight panic in my chest,
holes in my stomach—
i discard all rotting shit.

it is time to dismantle
this museum of mistakes,
toss the past into a bag,
present it to the trash man,
let it burn

i discard people—
all friends who eat suicide
day after day,
suck smoke, whining, "i can't i can't"
bitterly hating those
who can & do.
i discard those who let skies
fall on them, never blinking,
those who fight star logic
and dream magic with ignorance,
prejudice, pessimism,
those who fight this old friend's
blind love
with dreamkilling skepticism & lies

   i discard years of hateful lying

aunt irene

she listened to children
ever so intently
& gently spoke in return
to build up little people,
never tearing down.
she listened to children
& shared treasures & interests
with sincere awe & appreciation
& when they hurt inside
being with her eased pain.
she eased pain
without ever talking about it.

1st luv/TWO BOYS

we traded secrets & jokes,
laughed afternoon into evening.
you held my hand,
let me touch the pounding
of your big sweet heart.
we laid close together in dirt.
nothing mattered
but your mouth on mine,
my hands on your hot back.
we let midnight drip from stars
over that field
of sleeping black-eyed susans.

BOOKSTORE BITCH or: in Kansas you can't even *give* poetry away

Poetry scares her.

The magic & mystery in living
& loving elude her & she
always looks afraid, suspicious;
seems to resent those who embrace
life with a bear hug.
i've never heard her laugh or
seen her smile. she takes herself
too seriously. poetry doesn't
move her beady eyes
to tears or cause her pea
brain to expand. it doesn't
open that miniscule rural
mind in amazement or
enlightenment to read the
latest ideas or interpretation
of the human odessey.

she doesn't "have space" in her store
to sell or display poetry
but she can sell the hottest
fuck novels & hunting magazines
& all the latest unauthorized
biographies, the likes of
Vanna Speaks & other literary
gems, *Tiger Beat, Teen Beat, & Bop.*

it's okay to fill young girls'
bodies with lust,
to encourage young men to
murder animals,
to fill mediocre minds
with trendy drivel
but God in Heaven forbid that
we should improve their minds or
touch their souls.

ITEMS

1. the here & now

i don't care what
or who
i was (if anything)
in past lives

if i can't be
Richard Gere or
Tina Turner in
this life

i just don't care

2. bomb

tv is a bomb that
never explodes.
people watch intently,
desperately sucking up
something with eyes & ears.
they sit there as seconds
turn into decades,
decades turn into lifetimes,
the tv bomb ticking
eating time.

3. the reality of murder

dying is natural, but it hurts

it hurts people.
it scares us.
it hurts animals.
it scares them.

it is wrong to cause pain,
to kill people or animals.

it is wrong to kill
animals to eat or wear

just like it would be wrong
to kill people
to eat or wear

just like it is wrong
for cannibals
to eat missionaries

just like it was wrong
for Hitler to kill people
to make lampshades
out of their human
skin.

starfucker

(for billy)

how he bitches yet
he never gives it up,
little virgin starfucker
how he bitches
& dreams of sweaty hunks each night:
sneering punks
swaggering movie heartthrobs.
when no one's looking
he chains wrists & ankles to bedposts
crawls up naked, slick, larger-than-life
bodies, licks feet, ankles,
muscular legs, between thighs,
right to the living source.
little virgin starfucker
gets fulfilled to every capacity,
by morning, mirages evaporate,
dreams drown in hot frustration,
& sunlight
the sticky sunlight.

Wayne Hogan

last letter to a friend

i've failed our friendship

if in touching your life
i have failed to show you the poetry
pulsating under all our skin

if i have failed to pry
you out of that battered shell,
to show you the beauty,
the wonder, the mystery
in living and loving

if the singing joy in my heart
has not been contagious to you,
if i have not convinced you that
God's love is equal opportunity

if in 20 years my love for you
has not convinced you
to love yourself
to love all people
to love all creatures with a brave
unbending commitment

if my friendship has not brought
color, love, truth to your journey,
then i have failed

if my love has not been strong enough
to quench the dreadful hate in your bitter eyes

if i have not taught
you to touch the magic of life
without fear, without shame,
with all of the enthusiasm of a silly child

then i fear i have failed you
& ought to say goodbye.

karen carpenter

innocent and groovy,
she sang better than
God's angels,
better than Pat Benatar,
even better than Madonna.

her sweet smile healed scars,
her voice filled a void,
gently shooed away
every loss and sadness.
she coaxed lost children
back from darkness.

she smiled hope
into the future,
sang love into bitter hearts,
new life into tired
teenage souls.

joan baez

she gets ideas that
panic warmongers
and other greedy people,
ideas that could
kill a lot of death,
love that could save anyone.
she's bled for others,
seldom for herself.
in heaven she'll be singing,
pleading to convince God
to extinguish the fires of hell,
she will be distributing ice water
to all those pitiful
hot souls.

Letter to Joe in the Navy — April 2, 1987

This is just to say hi to you little brother
in California and to tell you i've been remembering
growing up with you when you were a young Capricorn,
a little goat ramming your way head-first through
childhood and me the proper little Virgo
sometimes getting you into trouble,
sometimes trying to keep you out of it.

remember how we played "Cowboys & Indians"
and you always made me be the Indians
(secretly i preferred it that way).
you had no use for my crayoned peace treaties,
much preferred to shoot me,
but when we played "Devil & God,"
i got to be God.

this is to tell you that i miss the rainy, snowy days
when we played with our toy people,
our treasure box full of little cowboys, Indians,
animals, doll furniture.

the furniture and animals were my domain,
i was in charge of town and civilization,
while you and your wild cowboys took off
for the hills in hot pursuit of Indians regardless
of how many times i told you the Indians
were here first.

this is to ask you if you remember our day-long,
red-faced bash-em-up fights when we'd pound
with all our tiny violent mights on each
others' backs, heads, faces, legs, arms,

the fight when you gave one of your ear-piercing
warhoops and leapt upon my back pounding like a
crazed bongo player as i held you up with one hand
to keep you from falling and cracking your head
on the sink and flailed away with the other hand
at your back and legs and anything i could reach
as hard as i could.

this is to ask you if you remember two happy, loud
and rambunctious little boys tumbling headlong into many
summers together before life got scary.

and remember how you'd trade your kingdom
for a piece of gum and often did.
i was always mean enough to take advantage
of you at home but fierce enough to want to protect
you from bullies in the outside world. now you've met
Satan worshippers and Nazis and you're not even
afraid of them. who knows what else
you'll be confronted with in your travels?
my playing God won't work anymore.
the concept of true evil is beyond your understanding,
you nonchalantly assume everyone is as highminded
as you were taught to be.

all i can do is sit here in Kansas
and pray my guts out for you and do.

now soon you may be on your way to the Persian Gulf.
there are things i've never told you.
this is to tell you that i am proud of you,
of your bravery and your commitment.
this is to tell you that i am afraid.
this is to tell you that oil and manifest destiny
are not worth my little brother's life.
if i could kidnap you and hide you i would.
there are things i've never told you.
this is just to tell you that i love you.

beyond sunday school

He seems like a
scary giant's giant
who can create life & death
out of boredom,
invent love when he's lonely,
hate because he's angry.

& then he seems like a child,
so primitive,
playing about with his planets/marbles,
exploding gasses,
pretty colors & sounds,
bigger than death,
throughout his playground/universe
space stuff pops,
flies, explodes, crashes
to his amused delight.
light years away from the scope
of any human eye
or comprehension
creation burns, freezes,
creates color & light,
changes,
remains the same
on Venus
on Jupiter
beyond Chiron

huge orbs travel given paths
minute by minute
eon by eon
as little bugs live & die
as we live & die
God plays

Wayne Hogan

election 1984

my friend, the 92-year-old
million dollar woman
votes a straight-line
die-hard Republican ballot
and has since Harding.

it pleased me to know
in 1984
my $0 Democrat vote
cancelled every conservative
X
she marked

1993

i don't want to
write poems
anymore
(except this one)
bcz all the words
in the world have
already been used
and if i make up words
some old harpy
screams
rulesstructure!
rulesstructure!
at me til
i just say
oh fuck poetry
& go do some
thing else

why i love to say her name out loud

(for Suzanne Nevels)

because it is a poem
in itself & she
is a poem likewise
without realizing it
the way she distributes
joy to each life
she touches without losing
anything   the way she
allows things to be funny
laughing honestly
& how she hugs God
& how He lives
through her

moon-in-aquarius poem

i am tame
civilized
like you
when i'm in public
usually in private
but i don't take it
as seriously as you do
i know it isn't natural

do you ever get sick of always
doing the right thing?
don't you ever get tired of
beauty, perfection,
and the pure wonderfulness
of it all?
don't you ever get bored
with always being
first, best, top?

isn't there a sneering
drooling primal creature
lurking inside you
needing to break out
(just sometimes)
to destroy the carefully
balanced law of it all,
the practiced protected tradition
by centuries of bland,
frightened humanity?

don't you ever want to go blazing
into the forests & fields on Sept. 1
with a gun in each hand
like Yosemite Sam
shooting every hunter you see
screaming, "Sport *THIS,* sportsmen!"

don't you ever want to go
on a rampage/crusade
destroying every television set
in the world?

to say "motherfucker"
out loud in church?

don't you ever want to
hurl yourself naked
off the top of a huge skyscraper
or mountaintop

searching for climax/meaning
for absolute anarchy

february 9

today was like having
a dispute with the
post office   arguing
with anything so stupid
yet so necessary &
powerful   nothing i
said was funny   spilled
coffee all over the
morning   felt late though
i had no place to go
any air i breathed
was wasted

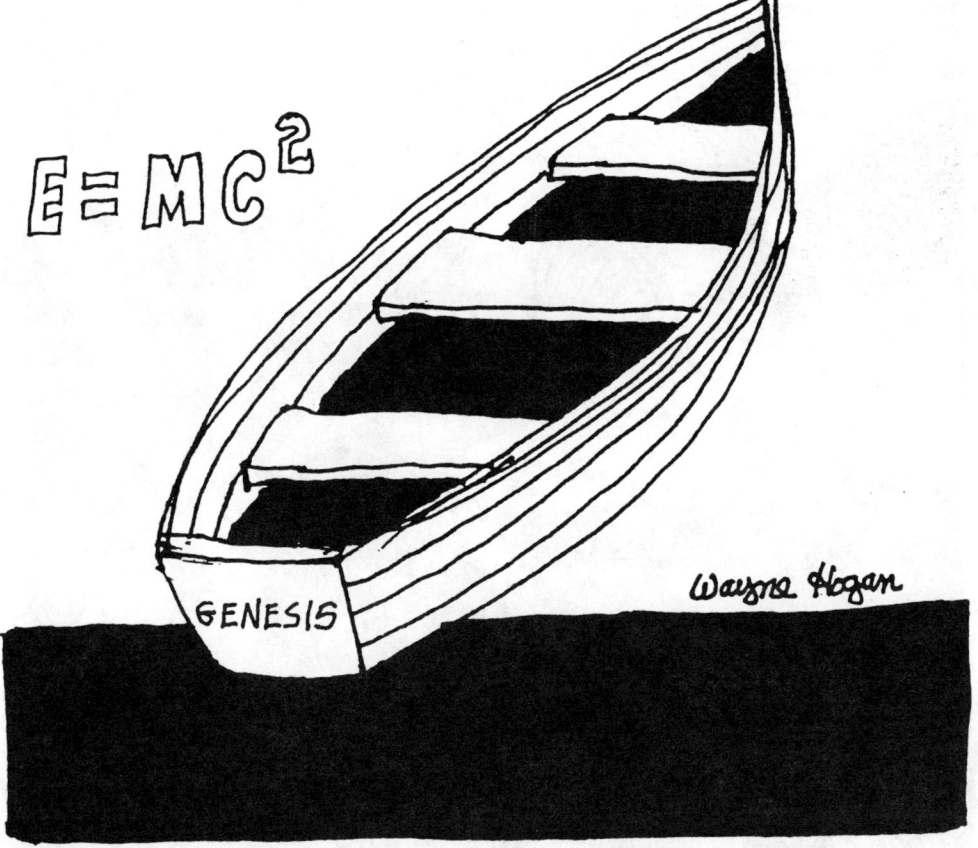

why

i was in my crapped-out
73 Nova, having just left Sonic
with a cheese pickle-o in one hand
& a container of ketchup in the other
both wrists firmly on the wheel
cruising home on Highway 281

i was thinking someone ought
to entitle a literary magazine
Why
because that's really what it's
all about — poetry, art, philosophy,
it's the little question at
the bottom of every big thought,
it's what we all want to know,
the question most people busy
themselves trying not to think about.

Biblical religions tell people
how we came into existence
through this big miracle by
a God who had the blues &
so he made us in his image
out of dirt without our permission
& they scream faith a lot
but they don't say
who made God or why

Eastern religions say that a gigantic sleeping
god breathes out, creating universes
& breathes in, destroying them,
each breath lasts billions of years,
& their Vedas explain every ancient truth
and wisdom but in 10,000 volumes
do they ever simply say
why?

Scientists also tell us
how we got here saying
in their vehement cocky way
that there is a logical explanation
for every occurrence, saying we
just exploded into existence &
can explain in detail
how we came to be but
those paragons of logic who say
there's a reasonable explanation for
every occurrence tell us
there is no reason why we exploded
into existence.

rules

1st you must realize
nobody likes you

2nd — if they say or pretend they like you,
they are lying
because you have something
they want bad
and they will do and say anything
to get and keep it

3rd — now it's up to you
to survive intact

memo

people are not freaks
or sideshows placed here
for your amusement
as you sit observing
frightened in your sterile
ivory tower

you don't know what they have suffered
or why they are like they are

people are individuals—
this is what creates
the color and variety in our world

it is wrong for you to sit
in your tower & ponder
why everyone isn't "normal"
& what you can do to
conform or "cure" them

people are not freaks
& the whole world
will not go to hell
for not joining your church

people are not freaks
put here to ridicule.
we are all equal in God's eyes.
it is not our job to judge,
it is our job to forgive,
to have compassion
for every life we touch
no matter what.

ABOUT THE POET

Michael Hathaway lives in St. John, Kansas with his parents, brother, sister, 11 cats, a dog, and Ratboy (who did return from the carnival). He is officially unemployed, but never stops working on *Chiron Review*, a literary magazine he has published since 1982. He has had poems in many small press magazines including *Pearl, Gypsy, Impetus, Atom Mind, one hundred suns, Raw Bone, Blank Gun Silencer, Abbey,* and *The James White Review.* He has served as chairman of the Great Bend Public Library's annual Poetry Rendezvous since its inception in 1988.

ABOUT THE ILLUSTRATOR

Wayne Hogan's poems and essays and short fiction have appeared in *The Christian Science Monitor, Abbey, Light, Atom Mind, New Mexico Humanities Review, School Arts, Mississippi Magazine, Cookeville's Finest,* and others. His cartoons and illustrations have appeared in *The Quarterly, Abbey, Light, Atom Mind, School Arts, New Letters,* and others. His first book of cartoons is being published by Alfred A. Knopf. Wayne and his wife Susan live in Cookeville, Tennessee.